AF322703

7 STEPS TO CREATIVE GENIUS

7 Steps to Creative Genius

Unlocking Your Artistic Potential

B. VINCENT

QuillQuest Publishers

CONTENTS

Copyright © 2024 by B. Vincent

All rights reserved. No part of this book may be reproduced in any
manner whatsoever without written permission except in the case of brief
quotations embodied in critical articles and reviews.

First Printing, 2024

Introduction

Grasping Innovativeness

Imagination is much of the time covered in secrecy, considered to be an unconstrained explosion of motivation that strikes the lucky few. Nonetheless, this view limits the immense scene of imaginative potential that lives inside every one of us. At its center, imagination is the capacity to see associations where others see none, to envision better approaches to being, and to take care of issues with development and knowledge. It isn't restricted to human expression; it pervades each part of life, from how we adorn our homes to how we tackle complex issues at work.

The excellence of imagination lies in its comprehensiveness and availability. It's anything but an intriguing gift given to a select gathering of craftsmen, performers, or essayists. All things considered, it is an essential part of human instinct, accessible to all who look to take advantage of it. The limit with regards to imaginative ideas and activity is implanted in our DNA, a device developed over centuries to help us explore and shape our reality.

In reclassifying imagination, we expand how we might interpret its worth. Obviously, imagination isn't just about delivering craftsmanship; it is about inventive reasoning, adaptable critical thinking, and the mental fortitude to investigate the unexplored world. It empowers us to adjust to change, conquer difficulties, and imagine a future that is unique in relation to the present.

By embracing a more comprehensive perspective on inventiveness, we pave the way for vast conceivable outcomes. We start to perceive the imagination expected in regular choices and see amazing open doors for advancement in everyday undertakings. This change in context is the most important move toward opening our creative potential, making way for an excursion that will change how we see the world as well as how we draw in it.

As we set out on this investigation of imagination, let us recall that it is accessible to everybody. It is an excursion of revelation, where the objective is definitely not a particular result but rather a more profound comprehension of ourselves and our ability to make. Whether you are a craftsman battling with a fresh start, an expert dealing with a mind-boggling issue, or essentially somebody inquisitive about the inventive flow, this book is a manual for finding the innovative virtuoso that exists in all of us.

The book's motivation and objectives

At the core of this book lies a basic yet significant mission: to direct you, the peruser, on a groundbreaking excursion toward opening your creative potential. This excursion isn't saved for the generally "imaginative" people among us; rather, it is a call to all who wish to investigate and expand their inventive limits. Whether you are a laid-out craftsman looking for new motivation, an expert intending to enhance your field, or somebody who still can't seem to be inventive, this book is made for you.

Our investigation is organized around seven key stages, each intended to stir an alternate feature of your imaginative self. These means are not simple speculations, but rather down-to-earth pathways improved with hard work, genuine models, and experiences from innovative personalities across different disciplines. The objective is to make inventiveness open, demystifying the course of imaginative creation and featuring its job as an essential expertise for critical thinking and individual articulation.

This book expects to accomplish a few targets:

Enlighten the Idea of Innovativeness: To grow how you might interpret what imagination is, move past the normal fantasies that keep inventiveness to creative pursuits alone.

Enable Through Commonsense Apparatuses: To furnish you with significant techniques and activities that encourage inventive reasoning and critical abilities to think.

Rouse Certainty: To assist you with conquering self-question and the apprehension about disappointment, which frequently block innovative articulation.

Develop an Imaginative Way of Life: To direct you in coordinating imagination into your everyday existence, making it an economical and enhancing practice.

Fabricate a local area of imaginative masterminds: To empower the development of steady organizations that encourage joint effort and shared development in innovative undertakings.

Toward the end of this book, you won't just have a more profound appreciation for your imaginative capacities, but you will also have a toolbox of techniques for taking advantage of your innovative potential. The excursion of opening your imaginative potential is both individual and all-inclusive. It expects boldness to start, tirelessness to proceed, and receptiveness to the heap structures innovativeness can take. This book is your encouragement to leave on this excursion, with the commitment that the way you track will be just about as interesting and rewarding as the inventive dreams you try to understand.

The Inventive Possible Inside Everybody

It's a typical misinterpretation that innovativeness is a gift, an uncommon quality given to a fortunate few sorts of people who beauty show stages, workmanship displays, and scholarly pages. This fantasy creates a shaded area over the huge scene of human potential, darkening the reality that the flash of innovativeness lives inside all of us. This book remains a signal, enlightening the truth that each individual has an intrinsic limit with regards to imaginative ideas and activities.

The idea that inventiveness is the selective area of specialists and masters isn't just deceptive but also profoundly restricting. It neglects to perceive the imaginative demonstrations we take part in every day—tackling issues at work, preparing a feast with whatever is in the cooler, or, in any event, conceiving ways of engaging a youngster. These are articulations of innovativeness, proof of our intrinsic capacity to imagine novel thoughts and arrangements.

Recognizing the inventive potential inside us is the most important move toward opening it. This acknowledgment starts with understanding innovativeness as a major human quality, one that is fundamental for variation and development. Our predecessors depended on inventiveness for endurance, contriving devices, making covers, and exploring the intricacies of their surroundings. This tradition of resourcefulness is important for our legacy, implanted in our DNA.

The boundaries to getting to our imaginative potential are frequently mental, resulting from long periods of molding and cultural messages that propose innovativeness is uncommon or unessential in specific fields. Conquering these boundaries expects us to challenge these convictions, to rethink being imaginative, and to perceive the worth of inventiveness in each part of life.

This book is a source of inspiration, encouraging you to investigate the profundities of your innovative capacities. It welcomes you to shed the limitations of customary meanings of innovativeness, to expand your viewpoint, and to embrace the likelihood that you, as well, can make, develop, and imagine additional opportunities. The excursion toward opening your imaginative potential isn't saved for the trivial few; it is a way open to all who will investigate the innovative pith at the center of their being.

Outline of the 7 Stages

Leaving on an excursion to open up your imaginative potential is similar to heading out on a huge expanse of conceivable outcomes. The compass directing this journey includes seven crucial stages, each intended to explore through the frequently supernatural domains of innovativeness and into unmistakable, available scenes where thoughts prosper, and advancements become completely awake. This part of our book fills in as a guide, offering a brief look into the territory we will investigate together, bit by bit.

Arousing Your Inward Craftsman: The excursion starts with a call to stir the craftsman that sleeps inside every one of us. This step is tied in with perceiving and sustaining your natural imaginative flash, empowering it to rise up out of the shadows of uncertainty and reluctance. Through functional activities and reflections, you will figure out how to recognize and saddle your extraordinary imaginative motivations.

Developing Interest: Interest is the fuel that drives the driving force of imagination. This step centers around fostering an outlook of investigation and request, training you to pose inquiries that open new roads of thought and disclosure. By turning into a 'thought authority,' you will figure out how to consider the world to be a perpetual wellspring of motivation.

Excelling at Perception: To make, one must initially figure out how to see. This step digs into the force of perception, a basic expertise for any imaginative undertaking. You will learn procedures to upgrade your perceptual capacities, empowering you to track down motivation in the unremarkable and see the exceptional in the standard.

Embracing Trial and error: Inventiveness flourishes with trial and error, the readiness to attempt, come up short, and attempt once more. This step urges you to get out of your usual range of familiarity, to embrace the untidiness of the inventive approach, and to find the worth in each endeavor, no matter what its result.

It's tied in with figuring out how to adore the cycle as much as the item.

Creating Discipline and Concentration: While inventiveness might appear to blossom with immediacy, discipline is its establishing force. This step stresses the significance of laying out schedules and practices that support your innovative prosperity, guaranteeing that motivation is definitely not a brief visitor but a deep-rooted buddy.

Teaming up and systems administration: Inventiveness isn't an island; it is a landmass associated with extensions of coordinated effort and local area. This step investigates the significance of imparting your inventive excursion to other people, of tracking down your clan, and of utilizing aggregate insight to lift your work higher than ever.

Carrying on with an Imaginative Life: The last step is tied in with coordinating imagination into the actual texture of your everyday presence, causing it to be a movement you take part in as well as a focal point through which you view the world. This step is a pledge to a way of life that celebrates and sustains imagination in the entirety of its structures, guaranteeing a deep-rooted excursion of development and revelation.

As we dive into every one of these means, you will be furnished with instruments, procedures, and bits of knowledge intended to open up your innovative virtuoso. Keep in mind that this excursion isn't straight, but rather recurrent, a constant circle of picking up, developing, and advancing. With each step, you won't just draw closer to understanding your creative potential, but in addition, you will develop how you might interpret yourself and your general surroundings.

Empowering the Imaginative Excursion

As we stand on the edge of this excursion to open your creative potential, it's critical to perceive that setting out in this way is both a bold and extraordinary demonstration. This last point in our presentation is a sincere support, a delicate poke to venture out with certainty and interest.

Inventiveness isn't an objective, but a constant excursion. It is a steadily developing interaction that moves us to see the world in an unexpected way, to part from the ordinary, and to embrace the excellence of probability. As you adventure through the pages of this book and draw in with the activities, reflections, and stories inside, recollect that with each step you move toward opening the imaginative virtuoso that lives inside you.

This excursion might test your cutoff points, push you out of your usual range of familiarity, and, now and again, make you question your course. However, it is at these times of vulnerability and challenge that innovativeness tracks down its most profound roots. The innovative strategy is as much about embracing the obscure as it's about making a genuinely new thing. It's tied in with figuring out how to confide in your capacities, to pay attention to your inward voice, and to permit yourself the opportunity to investigate, analyze, and express yourself.

Allow this book to serve as an aide, yet as a buddy, on your imaginative excursion. Inside its sections, you'll track down systems and bits of knowledge, as well as motivation and backing. Keep in mind that the way to unlock your creative potential is particularly yours. It will be molded by your encounters, your fantasies, and your viewpoint.

As you push ahead, clutch the conviction that imagination is an unlimited power, one that associates you with your generally credible self and with the world in a significant manner. Your imaginative excursion is a gift to yourself, but also to the individuals who will be moved by the work you do and the vision you share.

In this way, take a full breath, open your heart and psyche, and step without hesitation into the excursion ahead. The world anticipates its magnificence, and no one but you can rejuvenate. We should start this experience together, with the commitment that the excursion of inventiveness is one of the most rewarding ventures you will at any point set out upon.

| 1 |

Chapter 1: Awakening Your Inner Artist

Recognizing Your Creative Spark

Every ride starts with a single step, and the journey to awaken your internal artist starts off with recognizing your innovative spark. This spark is the innate capability inside you to create, innovate, and imagine. It's existing in the daydreams that whisk you away to imaginary places, in the problem-solving techniques you devise at work, and even in the easy act of selecting your outfit for the day. Creativity isn't always confined to portraying masterpieces or composing symphonies; it is woven into the material of our everyday lives.

To ignite this spark into a flame, the first step is to be well known and rejoice in your moments of creativity. This e-book invites you to reflect on your life and understand these instances, no matter how insignificant they may seem, and the place you have been creative. Did you discover a new way to prepare your dwelling space? Have you ever improvised a recipe with any components you had on hand? Or possibly you have discovered a novel answer to a business challenge? These are all manifestations of your innovative spark.

Understanding that creativity comes in many varieties is crucial. It's now not simply about the arts; it is about wondering differently, making connections, and expressing yourself in special ways. By acknowledging these moments, you start to see yourself as the innovative being you are.

To help you apprehend and domesticate this spark, this chapter offers techniques and exercises. One such exercise is retaining a creativity journal, in which you document your everyday observations of your innovative ideas and actions. This exercise no longer solely affirms your innovative capabilities but additionally makes you more conscious of the creativity that surrounds you.

As you embark on this ride of recognition, take into account that each super artist, inventor, and thinker started out with a spark. Your spark is simply as effective and holds the promise of monstrous innovative potential. By recognizing and nurturing it, you open the door to a world of inventive exploration and innovation. Let this be the start of a stunning experience to awaken the artist inside you—the place you rediscover yourself and the boundless creativity that resides within.

Overcoming mental blocks

In the quest to awaken your inner artist, grasping and overcoming intellectual blocks is akin to clearing the brush from a hidden path. These blocks—fear of judgment, perfectionism, and impostor syndrome, among others—act as barriers, hindering the waft of creativity and self-expression. The ride to inventive awakening requires us to confront these obstacles, now not as insurmountable barriers but as challenges to be navigated and overcome.

The worry of judgment can paralyze the innovative spirit, anchoring us in the security of the recognized and the tried. It whispers doubts into our ears, preventing us from sharing our work with the world again. Overcoming this concern starts with the recognition that all artwork is subjective, and each piece resonates in a different way with every viewer. Embracing the vulnerability of advent and viewing criticism as a device for growth can radically change worry into courage.

Perfectionism, meanwhile, is the excessive wall that surrounds the treasure of creativity. It needs flawless execution, frequently at the price of the pleasure and spontaneity of creation. To dismantle this wall, it is integral to undertake a mindset of exploration and learning. Recognizing that every "imperfect" strive is a step toward mastery and that real artistry lies in expression, not perfection, can liberate the innovative process.

Impostor syndrome, the shadow that follows many innovative individuals, casts doubt on one's capabilities and accomplishments. It's the voice that says, "You're no longer an actual artist." It's difficult for us to create. Overcoming impostor syndrome entails asserting your identification as a creator, grasping that each and every artist is on a trip of growth, and that artistry is now not a vacation spot but a path.

This chapter provides sensible workout routines and mind-set shifts to navigate these intellectual blocks. One workout entail writing a letter to your future self, describing your innovative ride and the fears you've overcome. Another method is growing "permission slips" for yourself, permitting you to make mistakes, to create besides judgment, and to discover new mediums besides the strain of perfection.

By addressing and overcoming these intellectual blocks, you no longer solely clear the direction to your innovative workable but additionally construct resilience and self-belief in your inventive journey. The system for overcoming these challenges is no longer a one-time act but rather a non-stop exercise of self-compassion, courage, and growth. As you research to navigate these obstacles, you will locate your innovative expression turning into extra fluid, authentic, and uninhibited, signaling the awakening of your internal artist.

Setting Up Your Creative Space

The house in which we create can substantially have an impact on the flow of our creativity. It's now not purely a bodily vicinity, but a sanctuary for the mind, the place thoughts can blossom and flourish. Setting up your innovative house is a quintessential step in awakening your inner artist, offering nurturing surroundings that can encourage and facilitate the innovative process.

This chapter delves into the significance of crafting a non-public innovative haven tailor-made to your unique preferences and needs. Whether it is a nook of a room, a committed studio, or a transportable kit, your innovative area must replicate your inventive identification and encourage you to discover your potential.

Firstly, think about the factors that stimulate your creativity. Light, color, and relief play enormous roles in shaping an environment conducive to creative work. Natural mildness can invigorate the mind, while the colors that encompass you can affect your temper and innovative output. Ergonomics is any other imperative aspect; a relaxed chair, a spacious desk, and the association of your equipment can have an impact on your capacity to focal point and create for prolonged periods.

Personalization is key to remodeling a house into an innovative sanctuary. Surround yourself with objects that spark inspiration: artwork that you admire, substances that excite you, and non-public mementos that join you on your innovative journey. This non-public contact can make your area feel like a reflection of your internal world, inviting you to interact deeply with your work.

The chapter additionally emphasizes the significance of business enterprise in your innovative space. A cluttered environment can lead to a cluttered mind, stifling creativity. Implementing storage options and preserving your equipment and substances can stream-line your innovative process, permitting you to focus on the act of advent as an alternative to the frustration of looking for what you need.

Moreover, the idea of a "creative threshold" is introduced—a ritual or bodily motion that signifies the transition into innovative work. This should be as easy as lighting a candle, taking part in a precise piece of music, or even the act of coming into your innovative space. Such rituals can help signal to your genius that it is time to shift gears into an innovative mindset.

In growing your best innovative space, take into account that flexibility and evolution are sections of the process. Your desires and preferences may additionally alternate as you develop as an artist, and your area ought to adapt with you. The aim is to create an environment that helps your creativity, conjures up your work, and displays your creative journey.

By investing time and ideas into putting up your innovative space, you lay a foundational stone for awakening your inner artist. This area will become a bodily manifestation of your dedication to your innovative practice, a location where you can explore, experiment, and categorize yourself freely.

Creative Rituals and Routines

The direction to awakening your inner artist is paved with rituals and routines that top your mind for creativity. These practices are now not about stifling spontaneity but about harnessing your innovative strength in a way that permits it to waft freely and consistently. This chapter explores how setting up innovative rituals and routines can serve as a bridge to your muse, reworking the elusive whispers of suggestion into a refrain of innovative expression.

Creative rituals are non-public practices that signify to your genius that it is time to shift into an innovative mode. They can be as easy as brewing a cup of tea earlier than you commence your work, arranging your equipment in a positive way, or beginning every session with a few minutes of silence. These rituals act as a psychological trigger, developing an intellectual environment conducive to creativity. By repeating these rituals, you give a boost to the addiction of coming into an innovative state, making it less difficult to get right of entry to your inventive flow.

Routines, on the other hand, give shape to your innovative practice. They are the scaffolding upon which your everyday innovative habits are built. This ought to suggest placing aside a particular time of day for your innovative work, dedicating sure days to one-of-a-kind elements of your art, or setting up a sequence of things to do that lead to your innovative process. An activity does not confine your creativity; instead, it offers your muse an everyday time and region to exhibit.

Incorporating mindfulness into your rituals and routines can radically beautify your innovative flow. Mindfulness practices, such as meditation or deep respiration exercises, can help clear your mind of muddle and decrease anxiety, creating a clean canvas upon which your thoughts can freely paint. Even a quick mindfulness workout before beginning your innovative work can notably affect your center of attention and openness to inspiration.

To assist you in setting up your very own rituals and routines, this chapter offers a variety of workouts and tips tailor-made to specific innovative disciplines and lifestyles. Whether you are a morning man or woman who prospers in the quiet of sunrise or a night owl stimulated by the stillness of the night, there are techniques to suit your herbal rhythms. Experimentation is encouraged; the intention is to locate what works well for you and grasp that your wants and preferences might also evolve over time.

Finally, the chapter underscores the significance of flexibility and forgiveness in preserving your rituals and routines. There will be days when lifestyles intervene, and your cautiously crafted plans may additionally be upended. When this happens, it is essential to deal with yourself with kindness, no longer view it as a failure but as a section of the ebb and go with the flow of the innovative process. Resilience lies in returning to your rituals and routines time and again, with the appreciation that every day gives a new probability for innovative exploration.

By embracing innovative rituals and routines, you set up a basis for regular creative practice, inviting your internal artist to emerge and thrive. These practices are now not simply about producing work; they're about cultivating an innovative life, the place the act of introduction turns into as herbal and integral as breathing.

Mindfulness and creativity

In the symphony of creativity, mindfulness is the quiet observer that resonates deeply, enriching each melody and concord with its presence. It's the artwork of being entirely existing and engaged with the moment—a nation of recognition that can extensively extend your innovative capabilities. This chapter explores the profound relationship between mindfulness and creativity, supplying insights and practices to help you harness this effective connection in your creative journey.

Mindfulness practices, such as meditation, deep breathing, and conscious observation, motivate a state of open, non-judgmental awareness. This country is fertile ground for creativity, as it clears the intellectual muddle that frequently obscures our internal vision, permitting clean thoughts and views to emerge. By quieting the regular chatter of the mind, you create space for your innovative muse to speak.

Engaging in mindfulness can additionally beautify your potential to study the world around you with sparkling eyes. Artists, writers, and creators of all sorts depend on their observational competencies to draw proposals from their environment. Mindfulness sharpens these skills, enabling you to see the magnificent in the ordinary, to find splendor in the mundane, and to translate these discoveries into your innovative work.

One of the biggest advantages of mindfulness as an innovative technique is its capability to decrease anxiety and fear—emotions that can appreciably avoid creativity. The concern of judgment, the strain to perform, and the internal critic can all be quieted through mindfulness practices. By fostering an experience of internal peace and acceptance, mindfulness permits you to approach your innovative endeavors with self-belief and openness.

This chapter presents a determination of mindfulness workout routines tailor-made for innovative individuals. From easy respiration strategies that can be achieved at your desk to sensory walks designed to heighten your grasp of your surroundings, these practices are designed to match into your daily routine, improving your innovative system without requiring hours of commitment.

Additionally, the chapter delves into the thought of "flow," a nation of deep immersion and engagement in an activity. Mindfulness is the key to unlocking this state, where time appears to stand still, and creativity flows effortlessly. By cultivating mindfulness, you can simply get into this state, experiencing the pleasure and achievement that come with being absolutely engrossed in your innovative work.

In embracing mindfulness, you are now not simply improving your capability for creativity; you are additionally embarking on a ride towards greater self-awareness and fulfillment. Mindfulness teaches you to admire the technique as much as the product and to discover pleasure in the act of introduction itself. As you combine these practices into your life, you will find out that mindfulness is no longer simply a device for creativity; it is a way of living, a route to experiencing the world in its full richness and depth, and a potential to unlock the full potential of your internal artist.

| **2** |

Chapter 2: Cultivating Curiosity

The Role of Curiosity in Creativity

Curiosity is the spark that ignites the flame of creativity. It is an innate force that compels us to explore, question, and marvel at the world around us. In this chapter, we delve into the imperative function curiosity performs in fostering innovative questioning and innovation. Curiosity is more than simply a desire to learn; it is a way of engaging with the world, a lens through which we can find out new chances and unearth hidden potential.

At the coronary heart of each innovative leap forward lies a question—a second of curiosity that challenges the status quo or seeks to apprehend the world from a sparkling perspective. The testimonies of exquisite inventors, artists, and thinkers are replete with situations where a single curious inquiry paved the way for modern ideas. Whether it was once Newton thinking about the fall of an apple or Da Vinci exploring the intricacies of the human form, curiosity used to be the beginning factor of their trip towards discovery.

To domesticate an innovative mindset, we ought to first nurture our curiosity. This starts off by permitting ourselves the freedom to discover, except for the constraints of immediate utility or efficiency. It's about embracing the unknown, venturing into unfamiliar territory, and discovering pleasure in the method of discovery. By fostering a sense of wonder about the world, we open ourselves up to a large expanse of thoughts and inspirations that can fuel our innovative endeavors.

Encouraging readers to undertake a curiosity-driven strategy to existence entails rekindling that childlike feel of surprise we all as soon as possessed. It's about staring at the world with clean eyes, asking questions about the commonplace, and now not taking the world for granted. This chapter gives sensible advice on how to domesticate this mindset, such as guidelines on turning into extra observant, getting to know to recognize the splendor in the details, and making an aware effort to step outside of one's mental remedy zone.

Moreover, we discover how curiosity can be systematically built into your day-to-day routine. This can be performed through easy practices such as dedicating time every day to study something new, engaging in conversations with human beings from numerous backgrounds and disciplines, and challenging oneself to clear up troubles in novel ways. By making curiosity a habit, we can always fill up the wellspring of thoughts and inspirations that feed our innovative work.

In conclusion, curiosity is no longer simply a trait of the innovative elite; it is an imperative issue of the human race that every one of us can cultivate. It is the key that unlocks the door to imagination and leads us down the course of innovative exploration and innovation. By embracing curiosity, we embark on a lifelong ride of gaining knowledge and discovery, where every query answered opens the door to a thousand more. Let us, therefore, domesticate curiosity with zeal, for it is the very gas that powers the engine of creativity.

Becoming an Idea Collector

The experience of creativity is richly paved with a series of ideas —fragments of thoughts, observations, and inspirations that we collect from the world around us. This chapter delves into the transformative exercise of turning into a thinking collector, a curator of curiosity who finds ideas in the big tapestry of life. To domesticate creativity, one ought to first domesticate an addiction to collection, hoarding snippets of the world in a treasure chest of ideas.

Becoming a concept collector requires growing an attentiveness to the environment, to conversations, to readings, and to experiences. It's about maintaining your senses attuned to the whispers of notion that flutter through in the most mundane moments. This exercise is no longer in simple terms about shooting what is without delay applicable or at once beneficial, but about embracing a broad array of stimuli that could, one day, serve as the spark for an innovative endeavor.

The thought journal stands as a central device in this quest—a bodily or digital repository where these snippets of notion can be saved and revisited. This chapter guides you through placing up your personal thinking journal, emphasizing the significance of making it without difficulty reachable so that taking pictures of ideas turns into as herbal as breathing. Whether via sketches, words, photographs, or clippings, your journal will emerge as a mosaic of potential, ready to be pieced together into something new and extraordinary.

In addition to the practicalities of accumulating ideas, this area explores the attitude of openness and curiosity required to see the world as an infinite supply of inspiration. It encourages readers to step outside their ordinary spheres of hobby and comfort to discover disciplines, cultures, and thoughts that at first might also appear unrelated to their innovative pursuits. This cross-pollination of standards is where actual innovation frequently stems from—a serendipitous collision of disparate ideas.

Strategies for enriching your thought series are additionally discussed, from leveraging technological know-how to seize and arrange thoughts to attractive things to do mainly designed to generate new ideas, such as brainstorming sessions, idea mapping, and innovative prompts. The chapter emphasizes the significance of now not simply amassing thoughts but revisiting and reflecting on them regularly. This manner of reflection can regularly expose connections and probabilities that were no longer apparent at first, reworking uncooked proposals into the seeds of innovative projects.

Becoming a thinking collector is an invitation to view the world with surprise and to locate pleasure in the act of discovery. It's an exercise that now not only enriches your innovative work but additionally deepens your engagement with the world. By cultivating the dependency of accumulating ideas, you make sure that your proper notion in no way runs dry, geared up to nourish your innovative endeavors with a wealth of possibilities.

Asking better questions

The artwork of creativity regularly starts off with a question. It's the spark that ignites the search for something more, something deeper, something undiscovered. This chapter delves into the energy of asking higher questions—those that challenge assumptions, open new pathways of thought, and invite exploration past the surface. In the realm of creativity, the nicest of the questions we pose to ourselves and the world around us can be the distinction between superficiality and depth, between acceptance of the status quo and the start of innovation.

Asking higher-level questions requires a shift from looking for immediate solutions to embracing the unknown. It includes cultivating a mindset that values the manner of inquiry as well as, if not greater than, the solutions that in the end emerge. This chapter introduces strategies to enhance this questioning mindset, encouraging readers to see each question as a probability to discover new territories of thought.

One key component included is the method of reframing problems. Often, the way a hassle is introduced limits the scope of practicable solutions. By mastering the ability to reframe problems, we can open up a wider array of probabilities and find options that have been previously obscured through our preliminary assumptions. This part affords sensible workout routines to exercise reframing, such as rewriting hassle statements from special views and difficult the underlying assumptions of daily challenges.

The chapter additionally emphasizes the significance of divergent questioning in asking higher questions. Divergent wondering lets us generate more than one solution to a single question, encouraging a breadth of exploration over depth. Techniques such as idea mapping and brainstorming are explored, with instructions on how to use these strategies to generate a variety of questions that can lead to sudden insights.

To foster an environment in which higher questions can flourish, this part presents recommendations on growing spaces—both bodily and mental—that motivate open-ended exploration and free association. This consists of guidelines on how to domesticate curiosity in everyday life, such as being attractive to various fields of knowledge, in search of new experiences, and deliberately putting oneself in conditions that present perspectives.

Finally, the chapter underscores the transformative conceivable of asking higher questions, now not simply in the realm of creativity but in all factors of life. By turning into adept questioners, we now not only beautify our innovative competencies but additionally deepen our appreciation of the world and our location within it. Asking higher questions is an invitation to trip deeper into the mysteries of life, armed with the understanding that the solutions we locate are regularly fashioned by way of the questions we dare to ask.

Exploring the World Around You

In the tapestry of creativity, every thread is a pathway leading to new vistas, new sounds, and new horizons. The act of exploration—venturing past the familiar confines of our daily lives—is an essential catalyst for innovative thought. This chapter is an ode to exploration, an information to venturing into the unknown in search of the gasoline that feeds the innovative fire.

To discover the world around you is to interact with it fully, with a sense of curiosity and marvel that transcends the activities of everyday life. It's about permitting yourself to be drawn to the unfamiliar and looking for experiences that challenge your perceptions and push the boundaries of your understanding. This may want to suggest traveling to far-off lands, immersing yourself in cultures vastly distinctive from your own, or it ought to be as easy as taking a unique route on your morning walk, opening your senses to the sights, sounds, and smells you commonly omit by way of barring notice.

This chapter encourages you to emerge as an explorer in your personal life, supplying sensible guidelines for how to infuse your everyday activities with moments of discovery. It discusses the significance of being current and conscious in new situations, permitting yourself to take in and analyze the variety of experiences the world has to offer. From attending workshops and lectures on matters outside your area to experimenting with new creative mediums, the chapter affords a myriad of approaches to developing your innovative horizons.

The idea of cultural exploration is additionally a key focus, highlighting how attractive one-of a kind culture can supply sparkling views and encourage new ideas. This area consists of guidelines on how to approach cultural exploration respectfully and ethically, emphasizing the significance of listening, learning, and acknowledging the richness of diversity.

Additionally, the chapter delves into the function of science in exploration. In an age where the world is at our fingertips, it discusses how digital equipment and structures can be used to find out new ideas, join innovative communities, and get admission to a wealth of expertise and inspiration. However, it additionally cautions against becoming too reliant on digital exploration, advocating for a balance between digital and real-world experiences.

Exploring the world around you is an invitation to step outside your comfort zone and embody the unknown. It's a ride that now not solely enriches your innovative exercise but additionally deepens your connection to the world and its myriad cultures, landscapes, and stories. By opening yourself up to new experiences, you permit the winds of exploration to raise you towards uncharted territories of creativity, where the chances are boundless and the manageable for discovery is limitless.

Creative Cross-Training

In the realm of creativity, variety is no longer simply an asset; it is a necessity. The notion of innovative cross-training, borrowing from the athletic world, where athletes teach in more than one discipline to enhance their universal performance, is an effective method for improving your innovative muscles. This chapter explores how a range of innovative things to do can support your foremost innovative endeavors, enrich your perspective, and lead to groundbreaking innovations.

Creative cross-training is predicated on the thought that creativity is an accepted talent that transcends precise disciplines. Just as a runner would possibly swim to construct patience and flexibility, an artist can write, or a musician can paint to release new dimensions of their innovative expression. This cross-disciplinary exploration fosters a greater holistic approach to creativity, encouraging the synthesis of thoughts and strategies from one realm to another.

This part provides realistic recommendations on how to include innovative cross-training in your routine. It starts off evolving by encouraging you to become aware of areas in your backyard that are your foremost innovative pastimes that intrigue you. These do not have to be far-flung from your contemporary skills; they without a doubt want to provide a sparkling standpoint and a new set of challenges. For example, an image fashion designer would possibly take up pottery, or a creator may experiment with dance. The key is openness to the training these new disciplines can provide.

The chapter additionally highlights tales of people who have efficiently utilized capabilities from one location of their lives to another, demonstrating the transformative energy of this approach. These anecdotes serve as both a concept and a proof of concept, displaying that the boundaries between innovative domains are regularly more permeable than we would possibly think.

Moreover, the dialogue extends to the cognitive advantages of innovative cross-training. Engaging in more than one innovative thing to do can improve problem-solving skills, improve cognitive flexibility, and even enhance intellectual health. By developing your intelligence in different ways, you are no longer simply getting to know new skills; you are additionally constructing a more agile and resilient, innovative mind.

To guide your experience into innovative cross-training, this chapter consists of a range of workout routines designed to assist you in testing new innovative practices. These workout routines are structured to be accessible, regardless of your beginning talent level, and are aimed at sparking curiosity and pleasure in the technique of exploration.

Creative cross-training is an invitation to break down the silos that regularly constrain our innovative practices. It's a name to discover the sizeable panorama of human expression and to locate connections where none appeared to exist. By cultivating an exercise that spans a couple of innovative disciplines, you no longer solely decorate your capabilities but additionally deepen your appreciation of the interconnectedness of all innovative endeavors. In the end, innovative cross-training is no longer simply about turning into a higher artist, writer, musician, or designer; it is about turning into an extra-well-rounded creator, successful in drawing proposals from the wealthy tapestry of the world's innovative traditions.

| 3 |

Chapter 3: Mastering the Art of Observation

Seeing with New Eyes

At the core of each innovative undertaking lies the artwork of observation. It's the potential to see the world no longer simply as it is, but however it ought to be. This chapter delves into the transformative energy of observation, an ability that, when mastered, can release a wellspring of notions from the most sudden places. To simply study is to see with new eyes—to discover the layers, textures, and testimonies that weave through the tapestry of everyday life.

Enhancing your observational competencies starts off with a shift in perspective. It requires stepping back from the ordinary way of seeing the world, which is frequently superficial and distracted, to an extra deliberate and attentive mode of engagement. This chapter introduces strategies designed to sharpen your potential to observe. These encompass practices like slowing down your tempo of life, even if simply for a few moments each day, to genuinely seem to be in your surroundings; altering your routines to expose yourself to new stimuli; and consciously directing your interest to small print that you would usually overlook.

Mindfulness plays a critical role in this process. By cultivating mindfulness, you learn to be totally present in the moment, which is necessary for deep observation. Mindfulness practices, such as centered breathing or mindful walking, can help quiet the mind, making it easier for you to be aware of the important points of your environment. This chapter gives easy mindfulness workout routines that can be seamlessly built into your day-to-day routine, improving your potential to have a look at the world around you with clean eyes.

Observation is now not simply about seeing; it is about connecting with your surroundings in a significant way. It entails the use of all your senses to utterly ride the world, going past visible aesthetics, which consist of the sounds, textures, smells, and even the emotional impressions of a location or object. This multisensory strategy for commentary can dramatically enrich your innovative palette, imparting an extra nuanced and vivid basis for your work.

To see with new eyes additionally capability to undertaking your preconceptions and biases, to appear past labels and categories, and to see matters for what they truly are—or what they may want to become. This chapter encourages you to exercise searching for regular objects, scenes, and humans as if seeing them for the first time, discovering splendor and thought in the process.

By getting to know the artwork of observation, you free up the doable to seriously change the mundane into the extraordinary. This chapter is your information for creating the observational capabilities that will fuel your creativity, educating you to see the world now not simply with your eyes but with your coronary heart and mind. Through the practices outlined here, you will begin to discover the limitless creativity that surrounds you, ready to be located and expressed through your special inventive voice.

The power of mindful observation

In the realm of innovative exploration, the strength of aware commentary stands as a beacon, guiding artists, writers, and innovators to deeper insights and richer inspirations. This chapter delves into the synergy between mindfulness and observation, a partnership that magnifies our capability to identify not simply the surface but the essence of our surroundings. A mindful remark is about enticing the world in a way that is totally present; the place every second presents a multitude of probabilities for discovery and creation.

Mindfulness, the exercise of being entirely existing and engaged with the right here and now, besides judgment or distraction, enhances our observational abilities by clearing the intellectual litter that frequently obscures our vision. Through mindfulness, we analyze to see the world with readability and openness, permitting us to seize the delicate nuances and complicated splendor that we would possibly, in any other case, overlook. This chapter introduces realistic workout routines designed to domesticate conscious observation, such as focusing on the breath whilst watching an herbal scene or enticing in a walking meditation, where every step will become a chance to note new small print in the environment.

These practices motivate us to use all of our senses in observation, going beyond the visible to encompass the sounds, textures, and even the smells of a location or object. By utterly immersing ourselves in the sensory journey of observation, we can find layers of that meaning and connection that feed into our innovative work. This multisensory strategy now not only enriches the innovative method but additionally deepens our connection to the world around us.

The advantages of conscious commentary extend beyond the enhancement of creativity. It fosters a sense of wonder and a grasp for the ordinary, reworking mundane experiences into sources of pleasure and inspiration. This chapter shares testimonies of how artists and creators have used aware remarks to smash via innovative blocks, discover proposals in unlikely places, and improve unique and compelling works that resonate with authenticity and depth.

To facilitate the integration of awareness into your innovative practice, this chapter offers a sequence of guided workouts and prompts. These are designed to be reachable and adaptable, appropriate for all and sundry, from the professional artist to the curious beginner. Whether it is looking at the play of mild on a constructed façade, the motion of humans in a crowded space, or the problematic patterns in a leaf, these workout routines have the intention to sharpen your senses and awaken a deep-seated curiosity about the world.

Mastering the electricity of conscious statement is a ride that can seriously change your innovative exercise and your life. It invites you to sluggish down, to savor the richness of the existing moment, and to find out the limitless wellspring of concept that lies ready in the easy act of seeing. Through conscious observation, you no longer solely beautify your capability for creativity but additionally domesticate a deeper, more significant engagement with the world around you.

Finding Inspiration in the Mundane

In the big panorama of creativity, the most profound inspirations regularly occur in the most regular places. This chapter illuminates the artwork of discovering the superb inside the ordinary, an ability that can radically change the mundane elements of everyday existence into a prosperous supply of innovative fuel. It's about seeing the magic in the mundane, recognizing the splendor in the banal, and uncovering the achievable in the prosaic.

The experience of discovering concepts in the mundane starts with a shift in perception. It requires us to appear past the initial, superficial layer of our daily experiences and to delve deeper into the textures, patterns, and rhythms that compose our world. This chapter introduces methods and practices to domesticate this shift, encouraging readers to view their day-to-day environments with curiosity and wonder. By actively looking for the unseen and questioning the overlooked, we open ourselves to a world brimming with innovative possibilities.

To illustrate this concept, we share tales of artists, writers, and inventors who have mined gold from the grit of everyday life. From the rhythmic chaos of a town avenue to the quiet contemplation of washing dishes, these creatives have harnessed their observations of the normal to produce works of top notch that have an effect on and resonance. These anecdotes serve now not solely as ideas but additionally as a testament to the transformative strength of searching the world with sparkling eyes.

The chapter, in addition, engages readers with a collection of realistic workouts and prompts designed to beautify their potential to discover proposals in the mundane. These things to do motivate exploration and experimentation, from documenting the omitted important points of an everyday trip to growing artwork from the patterns located in nature or the city landscape. The purpose is to improve a dependency on seeing innovative possibilities in each and every moment, turning the mundane into a canvas for innovation and expression.

One of the key messages of this chapter is the significance of presence and awareness. By thoroughly existing in our day-to-day lives, we permit ourselves to note and recognize the splendor and concepts that surround us. This attention can radically change regular experiences into moments of insight, sparking thoughts that fuel our innovative projects.

In embracing the mundane, we additionally embody a more sustainable and available strategy for innovative inspiration. We examine that we no longer want to challenge a long way or search for out the first-rate to locate our muse; instead, we find out that idea is all around us, ready to be considered and seized. By discovering notions in the mundane, we liberate countless wellsprings of innovative potential, one that enriches our work and our lives with depth, meaning, and beauty.

Observation Exercises

To grasp the artwork of observation—an ability foundational to unlocking the depths of creativity—requires practice, a lot like any other skill. This chapter offers a curated series of workout routines designed to sharpen your observational skills, turning the act of seeing into a deliberate practice. These workout routines are crafted to be enticing and accessible, supplying a pathway to enhance your capacity to understand and respect the complicated, important points and refined nuances of the world around you.

1. The Daily Detail: Begin with the aid of deciding on one regular object every day to have a look at it in detail. Spend 5 to ten minutes analyzing it closely, noting its color, texture, form, and any different characteristics. Sketch it or write a specific description. This exercise trains you to sense the richness of elements in day-to-day objects, cultivating an addiction to aware observation.

2. People Watching with Purpose: Spend some time in a public place, like a park or a café, and discreetly study the human beings around you. Notice their behaviors, interactions, and expressions. Imagine their stories. This workout now not only hones your potential to seize the essence of human emotion and interplay, but additionally evokes empathy and narrative thinking.

3. Nature's Nuances: Nature provides an infinite supply of observational wonders. Choose an herbal placement and center

of attention on a unique element—such as a tree, a physique of water, or a patch of earth. Observe it for a prolonged period, noting adjustments in light, movement, and existence inside this microcosm. This exercise encourages a deeper connection with the herbal world and displays the dynamic tactics frequently overlooked.

4. Urban Texture Trawl: Urban environments are prosperous tapestries of texture and pattern. Take a stroll through a town or city with the precise intent of staring at these elements. Notice the interaction of architectural styles, the put-on and tear on surfaces, and the graffiti's stories. Photograph or diagram what you find. This exercise opens your eyes to the visible testimonies embedded in city landscapes.

5. Sensory Immersion: Choose familiar surroundings and center your attention on experiencing them via one sense at a time. For instance, shut your eyes and focal point on the sounds, or listen to the smells. This exercise deepens your sensory consciousness and can lead to new insights about familiar places.

Each exercise is designed not solely to enhance your observational capabilities but additionally to incorporate commentary into your innovative process. By engaging in these practices many times, you increase the reservoir of images, sounds, textures, and experiences that can serve as uncooked fabric for your innovative work. Observation has now become not simply a passive act but an active, attractive technique that fuels your creativity and enriches your art.

Moreover, these workouts underscore the significance of normal exercise in creating eager observational skills. Just as a musician practice scales to enhance their musicality, a creator practices commentary to beautify their creativity. By incorporating these workout routines into your everyday routine, you seriously change remark from a fleeting pastime into a disciplined artwork form, opening your eyes to the countless ideas that surround you.

Applying Observation to Your Art

The proper essence of creativity frequently lies no longer just in the potential to study the world in all its elements and marvel, but in translating these observations into compelling art. This chapter serves as a bridge between the act of remark and the system of creation, presenting coaching on how to infuse your innovative initiatives with the depth and richness of your observational insights.

To begin, we discover the idea of a commentary journal or sketchbook, a quintessential device for any innovative individual. This is your private repository, where all observations—sketches, descriptions, photos, and notes—can be accrued and revisited. Keeping such a journal encourages not solely the dependency of a normal statement but additionally serves as a wellspring of notion when in search of ideas for innovative projects. This area affords realistic suggestions on how to efficiently keep a note journal, along with how to arrange your entries in a way that enhances their usefulness for your art.

Next, the chapter delves into techniques for translating observations into creativity. It begins with the manner of selection—deciding which observations are most viable for your work. This entails reflecting on what resonates with you personally, what sparks your curiosity, and what aligns with your creative goals. We talk about techniques to sift through your accumulated observations, identifying these gemstones that promise to enrich your innovative endeavors.

Once a promising commentary is selected, the chapter publications you through the system of thought generation. Here, brainstorming and idea mapping strategies come to the fore, helping you build on your preliminary commentary and discover a range of instructions your venture may want to take. This section is about broadening your innovative horizons, permitting your observations to mingle with your imagination, and introducing progressive principles and approaches.

The transition from remark to introduction is additionally a ride of experimentation. This part encourages you to test with extraordinary mediums and styles, using your observations as a launching pad. Whether you are a writer, painter, musician, or designer, the chapter presents recommendations on how to adapt and follow your observations to your precise medium. Real-life examples of artists who have masterfully incorporated their observations into artwork are highlighted, imparting each concept and perception into the innovative process.

Finally, the chapter emphasizes the significance of reflection and refinement. It encourages you to constantly revisit your commentary journal, no longer simply as a supply of proposals but additionally as a device for essential reflection on your work. By evaluating your closing creations with unique observations, you acquire treasured insights into your innovative process, research what works and what doesn't, and discover areas for growth and exploration in future projects.

Applying statement to your artwork is now not a linear system but a cyclical one; the place commentary fuels creation, and creation, in turn, deepens observation. This chapter is your information for making this cycle a central section of your innovative practice, making sure that your artwork is constantly vibrant, inspired, and deeply linked to the world around you.

| 4 |

Chapter 4: Embracing Experimentation

The experimentation mindset

At the coronary heart of each and every innovative recreation lies a spirit of experimentation—a willingness to venture into the unknown and include the myriad probabilities that lie beyond the familiar. This chapter delves into the essence of the experimentation mindset, a paradigm that champions curiosity over fear, mastering over success, and innovation over conformity. To without a doubt embody experimentation is to recognize that the course to creativity is paved now, not with a walk in the park but with the bravery to try, fail, and attempt again.

Adopting an experimental mindset requires a substantial shift in perspective. It entails seeing each innovative assignment now not as a barrier but as an invitation to explore. This mindset is characterized by an intrinsic faith that there is no such element as failure, solely feedback. Each attempt, every challenge into the new and untested, affords treasured insights that propel us in addition to our innovative journey.

The chapter explores the pivotal role of risk-taking in fostering creativity. It encourages you to step beyond the protection of what you comprehend and undertake into uncharted territory. This should suggest experimenting with a new artwork form, writing in a unique genre, or exploring unfamiliar subjects. The key is to push the boundaries of your remedy zone and grasp that this increase regularly happens at the edges of our experience.

To domesticate an experimentation mindset, one needs to analyze to embody the opportunity of failure. This chapter offers techniques to reframe failure no longer as a setback but as an integral element of the innovative process. It encourages readers to view every "failure" as a steppingstone, an integral phase of the experience in the direction of mastery and discovery. By learning to detach from the consequences and center their attention on the process, creatives can overcome the worry of failure that regularly inhibits daring exploration.

Moreover, the chapter discusses the significance of persistence and resilience in experimentation. The route of creativity is seldom linear; it is fraught with detours, obstacles, and lifeless ends. However, it is exactly these challenges that sharpen our skills, refine our ideas, and support our resolve. The experimentation mindset embraces these challenges, recognizing that every opportunity is a probability to learn, adapt, and evolve.

In conclusion, adopting an experimentation mindset is about more than simply attempting new things; it is about remodeling the way we approach creativity itself. It's a dedication to perpetual learning, to the relentless pursuit of innovation, and to the faith that the biggest achievements regularly come from the most surprising places. By embracing this mindset, we open ourselves to the limitless probabilities of what we can create, discover, and become.

Trying new techniques

In the journey of creativity, venturing past the familiar shores of hooked-up techniques and strategies is critical for discovering new territories of expression and innovation. This chapter delves into the transformative strength of attempting new techniques, urging you to step out of your remedy quarter and embody the unfamiliar as a catalyst for innovative growth.

The exploration of new methods is akin to mastering a new language—it opens up a world of probabilities previously unimagined. Whether it's a painter experimenting with digital media, a creator enjoying narrative structures, or a musician exploring unconventional soundscapes, venturing into uncharted, innovative waters can lead to breakthroughs that redefine the boundaries of one's art.

To motivate this exploration, the chapter offers a roadmap for integrating new methods into your innovative practice. It starts off with the easy act of curiosity—seeking out what intrigues you, be it a method you've admired in others' work or a medium you've continually desired to explore. From here, its publications you through the manner of getting to know and experimentation, emphasizing the significance of persistence and playfulness. Learning something new can be challenging; however, drawing near it with an experience of play can seriously change these challenges into fun discoveries.

Examples of innovative masters who have reinvented their work by means of embracing new strategies punctuate the chapter, serving as each concept and proof that stepping into the unknown can lead to gorgeous outcomes. These memories spotlight now not solely the successes but additionally the preliminary struggles, demystifying the procedure and reinforcing the message that boom regularly requires perseverance through discomfort.

Practical hints for how to weave experimentation into your day-to-day movements are additionally provided. This consists of setting aside dedicated time for exploration, using prompts or challenges as a way to interact with new techniques, and becoming a member of communities or workshops where you can study and scan in a supportive environment.

The chapter additionally addresses the combination of self-discipline and spontaneity required in this process. While experimentation is inherently about exploration and play, coming near it with a positive degree of discipline—setting goals, persisting through difficulties, and reflecting on your progress—can beautify the journey and the consequences of your exploratory efforts.

In embracing new techniques, you no longer solely amplify your innovative toolkit but additionally deepen your grasp of your very own abilities and preferences. This experience of exploration and discovery is now not simply about discovering new methods to specify your ideas; it's about finding new elements of yourself as a creator. By attempting new techniques, you open the door to a world of innovative possibilities, inviting innovation and sparkling ideas into your work.

Creative problem solving

The coronary heart of creativity frequently beats strongest in the face of challenges; the desire for options beckons the thinking to assignment past traditional boundaries. This chapter explores the essence of innovative troubleshooting, offering experimentation now not purely as a device for creative expression but as a quintessential approach for overcoming innovative obstacles. It posits that the most revolutionary options regularly emerge from a willingness to interact with the unknown and to query the status quo.

Creative troubleshooting is depicted as a dynamic procedure that starts with a clear identification of the mission at hand. Rather than speeding toward a solution, the chapter encourages a step back, advocating for a period of reflection and inquiry. It's in this house that experimentation will become an effective ally, providing the capacity to discover a multitude of avenues and chances that traditional methods may overlook.

Strategies for brainstorming and ideation are introduced as the lifeblood of this exploratory phase. Divergent thinking—the capacity to suppose in assorted and unconventional directions—is championed here. Readers are guided through workouts designed to expand their problem-solving repertoire, encouraging the exploration of as many options as feasible besides immediate judgment or dismissal. Techniques such as idea mapping, SCAMPER (substitute, combine, adapt, modify, put to some other use, eliminate, reverse), and the "Five Whys" technique are detailed, providing a structured strategy for unleashing innovative potential.

The narrative then shifts to the idea of innovative constraints. Far from being barriers to creativity, barriers are reimagined as catalysts for innovation. The chapter elucidates how self-imposed constraints or embracing exterior barriers can sharpen focal points and foster innovative options that would possibly no longer have been located in a more permissive environment. Examples from records and modern exercise where constraints have led to groundbreaking innovative achievements are woven throughout, illustrating the precept in action.

In the experience from trouble identification to solution, the chapter emphasizes the significance of experimentation and iteration. It advocates for a cycle of prototyping, testing, and refining, where every new release brings readability and closer alignment with the supposed goal. This iterative technique is introduced no longer as a linear course but as a spiral, where every cycle of experimentation deepens grasp and improves the innovative outcome.

Reflecting on the narrative of innovative hassle solving, the chapter concludes by reinforcing the idea that the most profound options frequently lie beyond the familiar. It calls on readers to include experimentation as a mindset, a method, and the ability to no longer simply resolve issues but seriously change them into possibilities for innovation and growth. Creative hassle solving, thus, is now not simply about discovering solutions but about redefining what is possible.

Documenting Your Experiments

The journey of experimentation is prosperous with discovery, learning, and, inevitably, moments of sudden insight. This chapter emphasizes the crucial role of documentation in capturing the essence of this journey, reworking fleeting experiments into lasting treasures of expertise and creativity. Documenting your experiments is no longer basically an act of record-keeping; it is an indispensable phase of the innovative process, imparting reflection, clarity, and direction.

Documentation serves more than one function in the realm of creative experimentation. Initially, it acts as a tangible reminder of the place you've been, what you've tried, and what results ensued. But its price extends some distance past mere memory. Through the act of documenting, you interact with your previous efforts, permitting you to seriously verify your work, recognize your thinking processes, and perceive patterns or topics that may additionally not have been obvious in the second of creation.

This chapter publications you by organizing a documentation exercise that enhances your innovative workflow. Whether through written journals, digital files, sketchbooks, or photographic records, the technique of documentation needs to resonate with your private fashion and the nature of your experiments. It discusses how to correctly seize each technique and the consequences of your experiments, suggesting that unique notes on your methodology, substances used, challenges encountered, and reflections on the technique are as essential as the last product.

Practical guidelines for developing a superb documentation gadget are shared, which include organizing your information in a way that makes it reachable and reviewable without problems. This may contain categorizing experiments with the aid of date, technique, or project and incorporating tags or key phrases to simplify the search and retrieval process. The chapter additionally explores the advantages of digital equipment and structures for documentation, supplying recommendations for apps and software programs that can beautify your record-keeping.

In addition to serving as a non-public reference, your documentation can grow to be a precious aid for the wider innovative community. The chapter touches on the electricity of sharing your experimental trip with others, whether or not through blogs, social media, or publications. This act of sharing now not only contributes to the collective information pool but additionally invites remarks and collaboration, enriching your innovative exercise with exterior perspectives.

The narrative culminates in the statement that documenting your experiments is an act of bravery and vulnerability. It requires you to confront your screw-ups and have fun with your successes with equal openness. Yet, it is inside this straightforward appraisal that an increase occurs. By diligently recording your experimental journey, you construct a basis no longer simply for private reflection but for non-stop gaining knowledge of and innovation.

In embracing documentation as a core issue of experimentation, you make certain that each and every hazard taken, each boundary pushed, and each failure encountered is a step ahead in your innovative evolution. Documenting your experiments will become a testament to your dedication to growth, a map of your innovative journey, and a beacon for future explorations.

Learning from failure

In the panorama of creativity, failure is now not simply a misstep but an imperative section of the terrain. This chapter reimagines failure, no longer as a cul-de-sac of disappointment but as a crossroads of opportunity, a critical aspect in the alchemy of experimentation. Learning from failure transforms it from a supply of discouragement into a springboard for growth, innovation, and breakthrough.

The narrative starts off with the stigma connected to failure in the innovative process. It argues that the concern of failure regularly stifles innovation, limiting creators to the security of the recognized and the tried. Embracing failure as an inevitable—and invaluable—aspect of experimentation opens the door to risk-taking and, ultimately, to originality and innovative success.

This chapter draws upon the memories of famed creators and innovators whose achievements have been born from the ashes of their failures. These anecdotes serve no longer solely as a testament to the resilience of the innovative spirit but additionally as concrete examples of how setbacks can be reframed and leveraged for future success. The narrative illustrates how many innovative breakthroughs are the end result of iterative failures, each presenting new insights and directions.

The sensible thing about studying from failure is addressed through a collection of reflective workouts designed to help readers analyze and extract lessons from their unsuccessful experiments. These workouts motivate a mindset shift, guiding the reader to ask the necessary questions: What can be discovered from this experience? How can this information inform future innovative endeavors? The chapter emphasizes the significance of retaining an experimental log, a distinct report of each success and failure, as a device for reflection and learning.

An essential theme of this chapter is the idea of "failing forward"—the thought that each failure strikes you closer to your innovative goals. It discusses techniques for keeping motivation and resilience in the face of setbacks, which include setting small, doable objectives, looking for comments and guides from the innovative community, and usually revisiting previous successes to preserve self-belief and perspective.

In conclusion, the chapter positions failure as an imperative issue of the innovative journey, an experience that, when embraced and understood, enriches the innovative process. It encourages readers to domesticate a lifestyle of experimentation, where failure is celebrated for its function in fostering discovery and innovation. Learning from failure is no longer simply about salvaging misplaced efforts; it is about constructing a more profound, resilient, and dynamic innovative practice. Through this lens, failure is no longer a shadow to be feared but rather a trainer to be embraced, guiding creators towards their most groundbreaking work.

| 5 |

Chapter 5: Developing Discipline and Focus

The Role of Discipline in Creativity

In the bright tapestry of the innovative process, self-discipline may seem, at first glance, to be an oddly muted thread. Yet, as we delve deeper into the essence of creativity, it will become evident that self-discipline is now not, in basic terms, a complement but rather a cornerstone to the flourishing of innovative endeavors. This chapter unfolds the nuanced relationship between self-discipline and creativity, dispelling the fable that creativity is completely the product of spontaneous inspiration. Instead, it posits that discipline, a way of stifling creativity, presents the fertile ground from which the seeds of innovation can sprout and thrive.

The coronary heart of this exploration lies in the appreciation that self-discipline in the innovative method is now not about tension or constriction. Rather, it is about placing a framework within which creativity can roam freely and safely. Discipline includes organizing routines, habits, and constructions that allow us to channel our innovative energies extra effectively. It's about making a dedication to exhibit up for our art, to face the clean page, the empty canvas, or the silent instrument, even when the concept looks distant.

This chapter introduces the thought of structured freedom—a paradoxical but amazing precept—that setting boundaries for one's innovative exercise really leads to greater freedom of expression. By defining certain parameters, be they time, space, or particular goals, creatives can sarcastically locate a deeper feel of liberation inside their work. The self-discipline of adhering to a hobby or a set of practices creates a predictability that the muse can be counted on; an everyday appointment at which creativity is aware of it is welcome and expected.

Moreover, the stability between freedom and self-discipline is cautiously examined. Too much freedom can lead to chaos and a sprawling panorama of unfinished initiatives and unexplored ideas. Conversely, too much self-discipline can lead to rigidity, stifling the spontaneity that breathes existence into innovative work. This chapter assists readers in discovering their very own equilibrium, recognizing that the finest stability is special to every man or woman and might also shift over time as one grows and evolves as a creator.

Through real-life examples of famed artists, writers, and innovators who have mastered the artwork of balancing self-discipline with freedom, this part illuminates the various methods by which self-discipline can take place in an innovative life. From the strict day-to-day routines of well-known authors to the ritualistic practices of eminent artists, these memories underscore the myriad varieties self-discipline can take, tailor-made to the wishes and rhythms of the person who creates them.

In conclusion, this chapter invites readers to reframe their appreciation of discipline, seeing it no longer as a barrier to creativity but as its ally. It encourages a proactive inclusion of discipline, no longer solely as a skill to decorate productiveness but as a profound exercise that nurtures and sustains the innovative spirit. Through discipline, we find the money for ourselves—the freedom to explore, to fail, to experiment, and ultimately, to create work that resonates with authenticity and impact.

Setting creative goals

In the ride of creativity, putting desires into action is akin to charting a route throughout an open sea. Without a vacation spot in mind, it is effortless to waft aimlessly, succumbing to the whims of the wind and waves. This chapter illuminates the significance of placing innovative goals no longer as constraints but as beacons guiding your creative voyage. It affords goal setting as a dynamic system that harnesses your innovative energy, focuses your efforts, and measures your progress, ultimately leading to a more pleasurable and productive innovative practice.

Effective innovative desires share positive qualities; they are specific, measurable, achievable, relevant, and time-bound (SMART). This chapter breaks down every one of these criteria, imparting a blueprint for placing desires that are now not solely aspirational but additionally actionable. Specific dreams slim your focus, directing your innovative energies with precision. Measurable desires provide tangible benchmarks for progress, permitting you to have good time milestones along the way. Achievable dreams make sure that your ambitions continue to be within the realm of possibility, lowering frustration and fostering a sense of accomplishment. Relevant desires align with your broader inventive ambitions, making sure that each and every effort contributes to your overarching innovative vision. Time-bound desires introduce an experience of urgency and momentum, propelling you ahead with purpose.

The narrative then delves into techniques for staying dedicated to your dreams amidst the distractions and detours that inevitably arise. It discusses the significance of flexibility, advocating for a willingness to adapt your desires as you develop and learn. The chapter affords realistic recommendations on revisiting and revising your desires regularly, making sure they continue to be aligned with your evolving innovative identity.

One of the central tenets of this chapter is the electricity of written goals. Documenting your targets solidifies your dedication and serves as a steady reminder of your innovative direction. The act of writing down your dreams is proven to considerably increase the possibility of accomplishing them, remodeling summary aspirations into concrete plans.

To bridge the hole between placing desires and attaining them, the chapter presents a range of equipment and techniques. From developing visible aim boards to using digital apps that track music progress, these assets are designed to preserve your innovative desires at the forefront of your day-to-day practice. Moreover, the narrative emphasizes the importance of accountability—whether through a mentor, a peer group, or a private journal—in retaining focal points and motivation.

In conclusion, this chapter champions the placement of innovative dreams as a necessary exercise for artists looking to navigate the complexities of the innovative process. By setting up clear, meaningful, and plausible goals, you now not only direct your innovative trip but additionally empower yourself to attain greater heights. Setting innovative dreams is no longer about limiting your creative freedom; it is about giving your creative direction, purpose, and an area to flourish.

Building a daily practice

Embarking on an innovative experience needs more than simply sporadic bursts of inspiration; it requires the institution of day-to-day practice—a consistent, devoted engagement with your craft. This chapter delves into the importance of constructing such a practice, illustrating how the rhythm of normal work now not only hones your competencies but additionally nurtures your innovative spirit.

The essence of a day-by-day innovative exercise lies in its regularity, not always in the quantity of work produced. It's about putting aside time every day to have interaction with your craft, whether or not for fifteen minutes or various hours. This dedication transforms creativity from a fleeting tourist into a steadfast companion, making sure that your competencies continue to be sharp and your connection to your work deepens over time.

As a useful resource in the institution of daily practice, this chapter presents realistic recommendations tailor-made to fit even the busiest of schedules. It suggests beginning with small, manageable goals, such as writing a single paragraph, sketching for a few minutes, or enjoying a few scales on an instrument. The key is consistency, no longer quantity; over time, these small everyday moves accumulate, leading to substantial growth and development.

The chapter additionally addresses frequent challenges confronted when constructing a daily practice, which includes discovering time, overcoming resistance, and dealing with innovative blocks. Strategies such as time-blocking your schedule, developing a committed innovative space, and using rituals to sign the beginning of your innovative time are discussed. These methods assist in creating a sense of pursuit and ritual around your innovative practice, making it less difficult to transition into the attitude wanted for productive work.

Inspiring examples of profitable artists, writers, and musicians who attribute their achievements to their day-to-day practices are woven at some point in the narrative. These tales serve as motivation and proof that a disciplined approach to creativity can yield high-quality results. From well-known authors who write each and every morning to painters who devote the first hours of their day to their art, these examples spotlight the range of each day's practices and the frequent thread of dedication that runs through them.

In concluding the chapter, the narrative emphasizes that the improvement of day-by-day exercise is a deeply non-public journey. What works for one person may also no longer work for another; the key is to test and locate what really helps your innovative process. Building a daily exercise routine is introduced no longer as an inflexible requirement but as an evolving, bendy framework that helps your innovative endeavors.

By committing to a day-to-day innovative practice, you no longer solely nurture your capabilities and abilities but additionally verify your identification as a creator. This everyday dedication acts as a consistent reminder of your dedication to your craft, fueling your innovative trip with purpose, discipline, and passion.

Overcoming Procrastination

In the mosaic of innovative challenges, procrastination stands as an especially insidious piece, regularly disguising itself as a benign prolongation, but subsequently threatening to erode the very foundations of our innovative practice. This chapter confronts the shadow of procrastination, unraveling its complexities and presenting techniques to transcend its grip, thereby safeguarding the sanctity of our innovative endeavors.

Procrastination, at its core, is a war with oneself—a conflict between the immediate remedy of avoidance and the long-term achievement of innovative achievement. The narrative starts off evolving via peeling back the layers of procrastination, searching to apprehend its roots. Psychological elements such as worry of failure, perfectionism, and the daunting nature of innovative duties are recognized as main culprits, each contributing to the inertia that hampers innovative productivity.

The chapter then shifts the center of attention to practical, actionable techniques designed to dismantle the obstacles erected through procrastination. Time administration techniques, such as the division of giant duties into smaller, extra manageable pieces, are introduced as a technique to decrease the crush that frequently precipitates procrastination. The institution of momentary desires and cut-off dates serves to create an experience of urgency and momentum, propelling the innovative character forward.

Further, the chapter delves into the electricity of our surroundings in influencing our propensity to procrastinate. It advocates for the advent of a conducive, innovative workspace—one that minimizes distractions and enhances productivity. From the business enterprise of the body to the curating of digital environments, the intention is to craft a putting that no longer solely conjures up creativity but additionally encourages the self-discipline to have interaction with it.

One of the most profound insights supplied in this chapter is the awareness that overcoming procrastination is no longer totally about bolstering productivity but rather about nurturing a healthier relationship with our innovative selves. Techniques such as mindfulness and self-compassion are explored as techniques to tackle the underlying fears and self-doubt that fuel procrastination. By cultivating a kinder, greater grasp strategy for our innovative struggles, we can gently inform ourselves and return to the course of productivity.

The narrative concludes with a call to action, urging readers to view the overcoming of procrastination no longer as a one-time fulfillment but as an ongoing practice. It emphasizes the significance of reflection, of recognizing and celebrating progress, and of constantly refining techniques to fight procrastination.

In the combat against procrastination, victory is now not marked by the eradication of procrastination, but with the aid of the capacity to understand it, apprehend it, and cross past it. This chapter equips readers with the equipment and insights to do simply that, remodeling procrastination from an ambitious foe into a manageable element of the innovative journey.

Focus Techniques for Artists

In the symphony of innovative work, preserving the focal point is akin to retaining the melody line amidst a cacophony of distractions. This chapter is devoted to the artwork of concentration, imparting artists a suite of strategies designed to beautify focal points and raise the best of their innovative practice. Here, the center of attention is no longer simply an intellectual workout but rather a cultivated talent that, when mastered, can considerably expand one's innovative output and satisfaction.

The narrative starts off by addressing the cutting-edge challenges to focus—digital distractions, the entice of multitasking, and the steady buzz of social media. In recognizing these challenges, the chapter no longer suggests a throwback from the cutting-edge world but instead provides techniques for navigating it with intention and mindfulness. Techniques such as the Pomodoro Technique—a technique in which work is divided into short, intensely centered intervals observed by way of quick breaks—are delivered as sensible tools for managing time and interest effectively.

Meditation and mindfulness practices are spotlighted for their profound capability to beautify attention and intellectual clarity. Through guided exercises, readers are motivated to domesticate a mindfulness exercise that fits their way of life and innovative rhythm. The chapter underscores the twin advantages of mindfulness: not only does it enhance focus, but it additionally opens the door to deeper tiers of creativity, permitting artists to tap into an extra-profound wellspring of inspiration.

The surroundings in which one chooses to create perform a pivotal function in the capacity to preserve focus. This part of the chapter offers actionable recommendations on designing an innovative workspace that minimizes distractions and fosters a sense of flow. From the corporation of the bodily house to the curating of sensory factors such as light, sound, and scent, readers are guided via the procedure of developing an exterior environment that helps their interior innovative process.

In addition to environmental and behavioral strategies, the chapter explores cognitive methods to bolster focus. Strategies for dealing with intrusive thoughts, harnessing the energy of visualization, and setting clear, motivating intentions for every innovative session are discussed. These cognitive tools are now not solely useful resources for retaining awareness but additionally decorate the emotional and psychological engagement with one's work, leading to more pleasing and innovative sessions.

The chapter concludes with an invitation to embody the center of attention now, not as a constraint but as a freeing pressure in the innovative process. It emphasizes that focus, when skillfully managed, does no longer restricts creativity; however, as an alternative, it amplifies it, permitting artists to dive deeper into their work, discover thoughts more fully, and produce artwork that really resonates. Through the practices and strategies outlined in this chapter, readers are outfitted to grasp the artwork of focus, reworking their innovative exercise into a more productive, satisfying, and profound experience.

| 6 |

Chapter 6: Collaborating and Networking

The Importance of Creative Communities

In the enormous expanse of the innovative landscape, communities act as lighthouses, guiding and illuminating the direction for man or woman artists navigating the frequently tumultuous waters of their innovative journey. This chapter delves into the coronary heart of why innovative communities are no longer simply really useful, but quintessential to the growth, inspiration, and resilience of those who are searching to express, innovate, and discover through art.

Creative communities come in myriad forms, each imparting special advantages and possibilities for connection. From the close-knit circles of nearby artwork collectives to the expansive networks of online forums, these communities provide a platform for sharing ideas, techniques, and inspirations. They serve as a wellspring of motivation, challenging and pushing every member to discover new horizons in their innovative endeavors.

The fee of enticing with a multitude of views can't be over-stated. Within a community, the change of thoughts through-out distinctive disciplines, cultures, and experiences enriches every member's appreciation and understanding of creativity. It fosters an environment where comments are no longer just welcomed but sought after; collaboration will become an effective device for in-novation; and assistance is effectively on hand in instances of doubt or struggle.

This chapter explores the symbiotic relationship between char-acter artists and their communities. It highlights how participation in a neighborhood can lead to non-public and expert growth, providing testimonies of artists who have determined their voice, honed their craft, and even catapulted their careers via neighbor-hood involvement. These narratives underscore the transformative strength of belonging to a crew of like-minded folks who share an ardor for creativity.

Moreover, the chapter addresses the challenges and rewards of contributing to a community. It encourages readers to actively par-ticipate, no longer simply as customers of the community's assets but as contributors to its richness and diversity. This may suggest sharing one's personal work for critique, supplying insights or recommendations to fellow members, or taking part in tasks that benefit the neighborhood or the broader public.

In conclusion, the significance of innovative communities is introduced no longer in basic terms as a side of the creative ride but as its very foundation. These communities provide a feeling of belonging, a community of support, and a worthwhile aid in forget-ting to know and inspiration. For artists navigating the complex-ities of the innovative process, discovering and being attractive in a neighborhood can illuminate the course to discovery, growth, and fulfillment. This chapter is an invitation to search for and immerse oneself in the collective electricity of innovative communities, to each make contributions to and draw from the proper collective creativity that binds us all.

Finding your tribe

Embarking on an innovative trip frequently feels like navigating an uncharted wilderness. The direction is riddled with marvels and mirages, making the agency of like-minded vacationers now not simply a comfort but a necessity. This chapter is an introduction to discovering your tribe—the neighborhood of creatives who resonate with your passions, share your challenges, and rejoice in your victories. It is in the midst of this tribe that you locate now not simply collaboration and critique, but an experience of belonging that fuels your innovative spirit.

The quest to discover your tribe starts off with a deep perception of your personal innovative identity. What drives you? What subject matters pervade your work? What are you searching for in the creations of others? Answering these questions sets the compass for your journey, guiding you towards communities that align with your creative ethos and aspirations.

In the digital age, the world is your oyster when it comes to discovering an innovative community. Social media platforms, online forums, and digital workshops provide unheard-of access to organizations committed to surely each inventive pastime underneath the sun. This chapter navigates the considerable panorama of online communities, providing techniques for attractiveness in these areas in a way that is both actual and productive. It emphasizes the significance of quality over quantity—the fee of deep, significant engagement with a select few communities over superficial participation in many.

Yet, the digital world can't utterly exchange the tangible connections made via face-to-face interactions. Local artwork collectives, galleries, workshops, and activities supply a bodily house to meet, share, and collaborate with fellow creatives. The chapter gives sensible recommendations on discovering these neighborhood resources, from leveraging public listings to tapping into the grapevine of the neighborhood artwork scene.

Integrating into a new neighborhood can be daunting. This chapter gives knowledge on navigating the challenges of coming into and becoming a lively member of an innovative tribe. It discusses the significance of contributing as much as you consume, of imparting guidance and comments to fellow members, and of being open to the equal in return. It additionally touches on the subtle dance of discovering your region within the mounted dynamics of a group, encouraging patience, respect, and empathy.

In conclusion, discovering your tribe is a fundamental part of the innovative process. It is through this quest that you no longer solely find out about a neighborhood of like-minded people, but additionally deepen your appreciation of yourself as an artist. This chapter is an ode to the journey of discovering your tribe, a testimony to the transformative electricity of the neighborhood in innovative life. It reassures you that, no matter how solitary your craft may also seem, there are others out there who share your ardor and apprehend your struggles—a tribe that awaits your special voice and vision.

Collaborative Creativity

In the realm of artwork and innovation, the fusion of minds can frequently illuminate paths that solitary exploration would possibly in no way uncover. This chapter delves into the essence of collaborative creativity, celebrating the confluence of various skills and views that can lead to exceptional, innovative breakthroughs. Collaboration, when embraced with openness and respect, turns into an effective catalyst for producing thoughts and options that transcend the boundaries of man or woman's capability.

The dynamic of innovative collaboration is multifaceted, involving no longer simply the merging of distinctive competencies but additionally the harmonious mixing of visions, work ethics, and personalities. It's a dance of give-and-take, where the success of the partnership hinges on mutual respect, clear communication, and a shared dedication to the innovative goal. This chapter explores the foundational factors of profitable collaborations, drawing on examples from a variety of fields—music, literature, visible arts, and beyond—where collaborative efforts have led to incredible achievements.

Initiating a collaboration regularly requires stepping out of one's comfort zone and reaching out to attainable companions with whom you experience an innovative kinship. The chapter affords instructions on how to methodically approach viable collaborators, from crafting a compelling suggestion that outlines the mutual advantages of the partnership to setting clear expectations and boundaries from the outset. It emphasizes the significance of alignment—not simply in terms of innovative, imaginative, and prescient, but additionally in work habits and conversation styles—to make certain the collaboration is productive and pleasing for all involved.

One of the central tenets of this chapter is the idea of "co-creation," the place collaborators interact in an iterative method of sharing ideas, feedback, and refinements. It delves into techniques for advantageous co-creation, together with setting up an everyday cadence of communication, the usage of collaborative equipment and platforms, and fostering an environment in which critique is welcomed and valued as a device for increase and improvement.

However, collaboration is now not without its challenges. The chapter addresses frequent pitfalls such as conflicts over innovative direction, imbalances in workload, and difficulties in decision-making. It gives realistic recommendations on navigating these challenges, together with putting up a clear framework for warfare resolution, making sure equitable contribution, and retaining flexibility in the face of innovative evolution.

In conclusion, this chapter celebrates the transformative strength of collaborative creativity, urging readers to include the probability of co-creating with openness and curiosity. It posits that through the act of collaboration, artists and innovators can push the boundaries of their very own capabilities, discover new innovative territories, and ultimately produce work that resonates with a richness and depth that is greater than the sum of its parts. Collaboration, in essence, is no longer simply a skill to be learned, but rather an experience of discovery, learning, and connection that enriches the innovative procedure and the people involved.

Giving and receiving feedback

The ride of advent is both private and communal, a course that benefits immensely from the views and insights of fellow travelers. This chapter delves into the subtle art of giving and receiving feedback—a manner crucial to the refinement and evolution of innovative work. It is inside this change that artists locate possibilities for growth, inspiration, and connection, reworking their solitary endeavors into a shared exploration of creativity.

The narrative starts off evolved via framing comments as a gift—a presenting of perception that, when given with recognition and acquired with openness, can illuminate components of our work. We might also no longer see ourselves. However, the change of comments is nuanced, requiring sensitivity, clarity, and a deep appreciation of the innovative intent in the back of the work being reviewed.

When giving feedback, the chapter emphasizes the significance of the "sandwich" approach—beginning with what works well, addressing areas for improvement, and concluding with fantastic reinforcement. This approach ensures that critique is balanced, constructive, and more likely to be obtained in the spirit of growth. The narrative offers recommendations for articulating remarks in a way that is specific, actionable, and aligned with the creator's objectives, urging readers to approach the venture with empathy and the actual wish to guide their fellow artist's journey.

Receiving feedback, on the other hand, is introduced as an exercise in humility and openness. The chapter discusses the preliminary emotional responses that can arise—defensiveness, frustration, even discouragement—and gives techniques for shifting past these reactions to interact with remarks constructively. It encourages readers to distinguish between subjective opinions and goal critique, to look for clarification when necessary, and to reflect on how the remarks align with their vision and dreams for their work.

The function of critique agencies and mentorships is highlighted as priceless boards for replacing feedback. These settings furnish structured possibilities for receiving various perspectives, fostering a way of life of non-stop studying and mutual assistance amongst creatives. The chapter outlines how to discover or create such groups, what to assume from these gatherings, and how to maximize the advantages of participation.

In conclusion, this chapter champions the change of remarks as a cornerstone of innovative development. It posits that navigating the complexities of giving and receiving comments with grace and gratitude now not only enhances the exceptionality of our work but additionally deepens our connections within the innovative community. Through the considerate alternate of feedback, artists and creators can foster an environment of collective growth, where every member is supported in their experience in the direction of realizing their innovative potential.

| 7 |

Chapter 7: Living a Creative Life

Integrating Creativity into Everyday Life

Creativity is now not simply an exercise but a lens through which we can view the whole tapestry of our day-to-day lives. This chapter unfolds the myriad methods by which creativity can be woven into the very fabric of our existence, reworking mundane duties into acts of creative expression and daily moments into possibilities for discovery.

At its heart, integrating creativity into our everyday lifestyles is about transferring perspective. It's seeing the manageable for artwork in the way morning mild filters through a window, discovering poetry in the rhythm of a bustling town street, or envisioning a story in the overheard snippets of dialog on a crowded train. This chapter explores how, with a little intention and a shift in mindset, each issue of everyday lifestyles can grow to be a canvas for innovative exploration.

The narrative delves into realistic techniques for cultivating this innovative mindset. It starts with the easy exercise of mindfulness

—being present in the moment and absolutely engaged with your surroundings. Mindfulness opens the door to seeing the tremendous in the ordinary, encouraging a country of regular curiosity and marveling about the world around you.

Another key method is to protect yourself from each day innovative duties that push the boundaries of your everyday routine. These can vary from writing a brief poem every morning to sketching something you see on your way to work. The aim is no longer to create a masterpiece each day but to construct an addiction to attractiveness with the world creatively.

The chapter additionally addresses the strength of play and experimentation in everyday life. It encourages breaking free from the constraints of "adult" conduct to rediscover the joy of play for play's sake—a nation where creativity runs wild and new thoughts can flourish. This may imply experimenting with new recipes in the kitchen, rearranging your dwelling space, or genuinely permitting yourself to daydream without guilt or aim.

Importantly, integrating creativity into daily existence additionally entails embracing imperfection. It's grasped that the innovative method is inherently messy, and that errors and missteps are now not disasters, but sections of the journey. This area gives alleviation and permission to be imperfect, highlighting that the splendor of creativity frequently lies in its flaws and unpredictability.

In conclusion, this chapter is a way to weave creativity into the material of day-to-day life, to stay creative as a substitute, rather than relegating creativity to simply positive things to do or moments. It's an invitation to view the world with wonder, to interact deeply with the mundane, and to seriously change the normal into a playground of potential. By integrating creativity into each and every component of our lives, we now not only enrich our very own experiences but additionally convey a special light into the world around us.

Overcoming Creative Slumps

Every innovative experience encounters its valleys—periods the place idea dwindles, motivation fades, and the as soon as shiny drift of thoughts slows to a trickle. These innovative slumps, while daunting, are an herbal section of the innovative process. This chapter addresses the shadowy geographical regions of innovative blocks and slumps, imparting a lantern to information readers via these difficult instances with realistic recommendations and psychological insights.

Acknowledging the hunch is the first step towards overcoming it. This area starts with normalizing the trip of innovative blocks and dismantling the stigma related to these durations of stagnation. It's essential to understand that even the most prolific artists, writers, and creators have confronted their personal battles with a void of inspiration. Understanding that these phases are brief, and cyclical can alleviate the strain and guilt frequently associated with innovative slumps.

The narrative then transitions into techniques for reigniting the innovative spark. One key strategy is altering your routine—stepping outside of your relief area can jolt your innovative senses awake. This may include altering your environment, experimenting with a new medium, or absolutely altering the time of day you interact with innovative work. Such shifts can provide sparkling views and sudden sources of inspiration.

Seeking new sources of proposal is any other critical method discussed. Inspiration can be discovered in the most unexpected places—from the tricky patterns of a leaf to the storytelling of a movie. The chapter encourages readers to grow to be innovative omnivores, ingesting a broad array of art, nature, and experiences. It additionally highlights the significance of feeding your curiosity through books, travel, conversations, and different enriching activities.

Allowing for relaxation and reflection is emphasized as a quintessential part of overcoming innovative slumps. Sometimes, the best direction of motion is to step again and give yourself permission to rest. This pause can be a fertile floor for unconscious processing, the place thoughts simmer and sooner or later floor with renewed vigor. The chapter discusses methods for reflective practice, such as journaling and meditation, which can help make your ideas clearer and reignite your innovative passion.

In conclusion, this chapter provides solace and options for navigating the murky waters of innovative slumps. It reassures readers that slumps are no longer indicative of a lack of intelligence or dedication but are actually phases of the innovative cycle. By adopting a proactive strategy to overcome these periods, embracing change, searching for new inspirations, and permitting for rest, creatives can emerge from slumps with a deeper grasp of their system and renewed enthusiasm for their work.

The Balanced Creative

In the bright tapestry of innovative life, preserving a harmonious balance between work, private well-being, and the need of creativity is both artwork and science. This chapter delves into the difficult dance of discovering equilibrium, emphasizing that proper creativity thrives no longer from relentless exertion but from a well-tended stability that nurtures both the artist and the art.

The narrative starts off by addressing the delusion of the tortured artist and the difficult concept that innovative brilliance is born totally from chaos and suffering. Instead, it posits that sustained creativity is nurtured through a balanced lifestyle, where rest, relationships, and exercise play as vital roles as work. This area affords a sparkling viewpoint on productivity, suggesting that time spent away from one's innovative pastimes can be simply as precious as time spent on them.

Strategies for accomplishing this stability are woven throughout the chapter, beginning with the significance of placing clear boundaries. Boundaries between work and rest, creativity and consumption, solitude, and socialization are fundamental to stopping burnout and holding electricity levels. Practical recommendations are presented on how to set up and recognize these boundaries, consisting of the use of science to put into effect work hours and the introduction of bodily areas committed to leisure and creativity.

Time administration emerges as an indispensable ability in the balanced creative's toolkit. This part delves into strategies for prioritizing tasks, setting sensible goals, and using equipment like calendars and planners to manipulate the finite useful resource of time effectively. The goal is to make sure that creatives can commit themselves thoroughly to their artwork at some stage in targeted intervals while additionally keeping adequate time for rest, reflection, and the joys of their backyard work.

The chapter additionally explores the idea of self-care as a foundational part of a balanced, innovative life. Self-care is depicted now not as a luxury but as a necessity for everybody engaged in the traumatic work of creation. This consists of bodily self-care, such as exercising and nutrition; emotional self-care, like mindfulness and therapy; and social self-care, which entails nurturing relationships with friends and family.

In conclusion, "The Balanced Creative" chapter gives a holistic view of the innovative life, one in which ardor for artwork is matched by a dedication to non-public well-being. It encourages creatives to view their fitness and happiness as imperative to their inventive success, advocating for a lifestyle were creativity and contentment dance in tandem. By embracing the standards of balance, boundaries, and self-care, artists can preserve their innovative spark over the long haul, producing work that is no longer solely more stimulating but additionally more sustainable.

Sustaining Your Creative Health

The ride of creativity is now not a dash but a marathon, requiring not simply bursts of notion but sustained vitality and wellness. This chapter delves into the concept of innovative health, a holistic mixture of mental, emotional, and bodily well-being that permits artists to interact deeply with their work over the long term. It posits that maintaining innovative fitness is as essential to an artist's repertoire as their technical capabilities or conceptual ideas.

Creative fitness starts with intellectual wellness, the bedrock upon which creativity thrives. The narrative explores techniques for nurturing a healthy mind, along with ordinary practices of mindfulness and meditation that can help clear the intellectual litter and foster a state of centered calm. Techniques for combating the frequent intellectual fitness challenges that creatives face, such as anxiety, depression, and imposter syndrome, are additionally discussed. The chapter emphasizes the significance of searching for expert assistance when needed, portraying remedy now not as a signal of a weak spot but as a proactive step in the direction of retaining intellectual health.

Emotional well-being is the subsequent pillar of innovative fitness addressed. The emotional highs and lows of the innovative method can be taxing, making emotional resilience a key attribute for sustained innovative work. The chapter gives insights into appreciation and managing one's emotional landscape, which includes recognizing the symptoms of burnout, navigating the complexities of innovative blocks, and cultivating an exercise of self-compassion and gratitude. It advocates for constructing a supportive community—both non-public and professional—that can furnish encouragement and perception on the innovative journey.

Physical health, regularly disregarded in discussions of creativity, is highlighted as a vital aspect of innovative health. The chapter underscores the connection between bodily health and innovative output, advocating for ordinary exercise, ample rest, and a nourishing weight loss plan as foundational to maintaining power tiers and intellectual clarity. Practical recommendations on integrating bodily exercise into the every-day hobbies of an innovative professional, from easy stretches to fight the sedentary nature of many innovative practices to hints for incorporating motion as a device for innovative inspiration, are provided.

The narrative then weaves these factors together, supplying a holistic view of innovative fitness that encompasses mind, body, and spirit. It suggests movement practices and check-ins as strategies for creatives to reveal and hold their fitness throughout these dimensions. Moreover, the chapter discusses the position of innovative fitness in improving the fine and depth of one's work, arguing that a well-maintained artist is successful in producing work that is no longer solely technically knowledgeable but additionally emotionally resonant and intellectually stimulating.

In conclusion, this chapter elevates the idea of innovative fitness to be an indispensable part of the innovative life, urging readers to prioritize their health as they would any other component of their craft. By embracing the practices of intellectual mindfulness, emotional resilience, and bodily wellness, creatives can make sure that their most necessary tool—their personal well-being—is preserved and protected, enabling them to explore, create, and innovate for years to come.

Looking Forward

The ride of an innovative existence is one of perpetual motion; the horizon continuously expands with every step taken. This chapter, "Looking Forward," is an invocation to include the future of your innovative ride with openness, curiosity, and a steadfast dedication to growth. It is information for sustaining the momentum of your creativity, for putting your sights on new challenges, and for being receptive to the sudden possibilities that lie ahead.

Central to the ethos of searching ahead is the precept of lifelong learning. The narrative emphasizes that the panorama of creativity is ever evolving, with new technologies, techniques, and theories continuously reshaping the boundaries of what is possible. Engaging with this regular flux requires a mindset of openness and a dedication to education, be it formal or self-directed. This part affords techniques for staying informed and inspired, from attending workshops and conferences to cultivating a variety of studying addictions that span genres, cultures, and disciplines.

Setting future desires is another focal point of the chapter. It discusses the significance of defining goals that no longer solely task and stretch your abilities but additionally align with your evolving innovative vision. Goal setting is portrayed no longer as an inflexible roadmap but as bendy information that adapts to the altering contours of your innovative landscape. Practical recommendations are given on how to set significant goals, measure progress, and pivot when necessary, making sure that your innovative trajectory stays bold and achievable.

The narrative additionally explores thinking in search of new challenges as a catalyst for growth. It encourages stepping past the remedy zone, whether or not via exploring new mediums, participating with artists from special fields, or projecting tasks that tackle complicated social and cultural themes. These challenges are introduced as possibilities to deepen your practice, broaden your ability set, and make a significant contribution to the broader discourse.

Remaining open to surprising possibilities is every other theme woven through the chapter. It highlights the serendipitous nature of the innovative journey, the place where threat encounters, unexpected challenges, and spontaneous inspirations can lead to some of the most profitable experiences and achievements. The narrative provides coaching on how to domesticate an attitude that is both proactive in looking for possibilities and responsive to the unplanned, making sure that you are usually placed to capitalize on the chances that arise.

In conclusion, "Looking Forward" is a name to view the future now, not as a faraway shore but as the subsequent step in a non-stop experience of discovery and creation. It encourages embracing the unknown with confidence, armed with the expertise that the skills, practices, and networks you have cultivated will guide you in navigating anything the future holds. By committing to lifelong learning, setting dynamic goals, looking for new challenges, and being open to the unexpected, you make sure that your innovative ride is one of limitless opportunity and perpetual growth.

Conclusion

Summary of Key Points

As we draw the curtains on this exploration of unlocking one's inventive potential, it is both reflective and forward-looking to revisit the trip we've undertaken together. This e-book has traversed the landscapes of creativity, delving into the mechanisms, challenges, and triumphs that form the innovative process. We've uncovered that creativity is now not an uncommon present bestowed upon the few, but rather a bright pressure inside every one of us, watching for activation and cultivation.

We started out with the aid of awakening the internal artist, recognizing that the seeds of creativity are sown in the fertile floor of curiosity and observation. We discovered that seeing the world through a lens of surprise and inquiry can seriously change the mundane into a canvas of infinite possibility. The importance of embracing experimentation used to be underscored, highlighting that the route to discovery is regularly paved with the stones of trial and error.

The narrative then wove through the significance of self-discipline and focus, revealing that the freedom of creativity is exceptional and nurtured in the shape of events and goal setting. This stability between spontaneity and order emerged as a central theme, illustrating that the dance of advent is most sleek when there is concord between the two.

Collaboration and networking have been celebrated as conduits for increasing our innovative horizons, reminding us that artwork is now not created in isolation but in the shiny trade of thoughts and inspirations with others. The ride then took us into the realm of sustaining our innovative health, emphasizing that our most treasured useful resource is no longer our brain or approach but rather our well-being—mental, emotional, and physical.

Each chapter, every thought discussed, serves as a beacon, illuminating the direction to a richer, extra-pleasurable, innovative life. These key factors are now not mere steps on a ladder but interwoven threads in the tapestry of creativity, each contributing to the energy and splendor of the whole.

In concluding this summary, let us elevate the appreciation that creativity is an ever-unfolding journey. There is no last destination, only waypoints of discovery and growth. The standards and techniques shared inside these pages are companions for this journey, guiding lights designed to illuminate your route as you proceed to discover the large panorama of your innovative potential.

Reflection on the Creative Journey

As we are close to the end of this exploratory voyage into the depths of creativity, it is crucial to pause and reflect on the trip undertaken. This second act of reflection is now not purely an act of memory but rather an imperative method of acknowledging growth, challenges surmounted, and instructions learned. Each reader's direction through this e-book mirrors the broader ride of creativity itself—unique, nonlinear, and wealthy with discovery.

The innovative journey, as we have seen, is inherently cyclical. It ebbs and flows, with moments of bright notion observed by using instances of introspection and doubt. This cycle is no longer indicative of stagnation, but of the herbal rhythm of inventive growth. Recognizing this sample in your personal journey is crucial. It affords relief in difficult times, understanding they are precursors to breakthroughs and evolution.

This chapter invites you to reflect on and consider your personal innovative milestones and the hurdles you have overcome.

Whether it was once discovering the bravery to begin a new project, pushing through a daunting innovative block, or opening yourself up to critique and collaboration, every journey has contributed to the artist you are today. Reflecting on these moments fosters a deeper perception of the experience and an awareness of your resilience and capability for growth.

The significance of persistence and resilience can't be overstated. The innovative direction is strewn with obstacles, both exterior and internal. Yet, it is the act of transferring forward—persistently, courageously—that transforms these limitations into steppingstones. Embracing resilience potential means viewing each and every assignment as a probability to learn, adapt, and emerge stronger.

As you replicate your journey, think about additionally the moments of joy, the cases of surprising inspiration, and the pride of seeing your thoughts come to fruition. These highlights are reminders of why we embark on the innovative route in the first place: for the profound achievement that comes from bringing something new into the world, from expressing our deepest selves, and from connecting with others through our art.

In concluding this reflection, consider that the innovative ride is as much about the method as it is about the destination. The experiences, insights, and transformations along the way are helpful treasures, enriching not solely your artwork but your existence as a whole. As you proceed to navigate the winding route of creativity, bring with you the training learned, the resilience built, and the pleasure discovered, understanding that every step ahead is a step into new possibilities.

Encouragement for Continued Exploration and Growth

As we flip the pages of our innovative narrative closer to the future, the route in advance is both exhilarating and uncharted. This chapter serves as a beacon of encouragement for you, the artist, the creator, and the explorer of the boundless landscapes of creativity.

Herein lies a name to arms, now not of battle but of bravery—the bravery to proceed pushing the boundaries of your imagination, to maintain exploring the depths of your talents, and to relentlessly pursue an increase in each stroke, word, and note.

Embarking on this perpetual ride of exploration and boom requires courage. It's bravery that comes from within, a get-to-the-bottom of that. Notwithstanding the inevitable challenges and set-backs, the quest for innovative expression is worthwhile and vital. This chapter celebrates that courage, reminding you that each and every innovative endeavor, no matter how small, is a step in the direction of gaining knowledge of your craft and deepening your grasp of your artwork and yourself.

The significance of staying curious can't be overstated. Curiosity is the compass that guides us through the sizable expanse of creativity, leading us to new ideas, techniques, and perspectives. It is the gasoline for innovation, riding us to ask, "what if" and "why not," pushing us past the familiar into the realm of possibility. This part provides techniques to domesticate and preserve curiosity, from embracing lifelong mastery to searching for concepts in the world around you.

Openness to new experiences is highlighted as a vital issue for growth. The willingness to step outside your comfort zone, to test with new mediums, to collaborate with others from exclusive fields, and to have interaction with unfamiliar cultures and thoughts enriches your creative palette. It broadens your horizons, no longer simply artistically, but personally, fostering empathy, understand-ing, and a deeper connection to the various tapestries of human experience.

Embracing the ever-evolving nature of creativity is additionally emphasized. The innovative panorama is in regular flux, formed with the aid of technological advancements, cultural shifts, and the limitless cycle of creative trends. Staying adaptable, inclined to evolve with the times, and open to redefining your inventive identification ensures that your innovative expression stays applicable and resonant. This adaptability is portrayed no longer as a compromise but as a hallmark of a mature artist who is aware that boom regularly capability transformation.

In concluding this message of encouragement, let this chapter serve as a reminder that the journey of creativity is infinite, stuffed with unexplored territories, hidden treasures, and possibilities for discovery. You are outfitted with the tools, knowledge, and resilience needed to navigate this journey. So, with your compass set on curiosity, your sails stuffed with the winds of inspiration, and your map etched with the routes of previous explorations, set forth into the future of your innovative voyage with self-belief and anticipation. The horizon is vast, and the probabilities are limitless.

Call to Action

As we methodically determine the end result of our ride via the nation-states of creativity, this chapter stands as a clarion call to action. It beckons you, the reader, to no longer purely be a passive tourist through these pages but to emerge as a lively participant in the unfolding story of your innovative life. This call to action is an invitation to take the insights, strategies, and inspirations gleaned from this e-book and weave them into the material of your daily practice, your inventive endeavors, and your private evolution.

Embark on this subsequent section of your trip with a dedication to practicing what you have learned. Begin by putting aside time every day for your innovative work and using the concepts of self-discipline and center of attention to forge pursuits that honor your craft. Challenge yourself to step beyond the boundaries of your comfort zone, experimenting with new strategies and mediums that can expand your creative vocabulary.

Join a neighborhood of fellow creatives, if you have not already, to share your journey, collaborate on projects, and provide aid and feedback. The cost of an innovative tribe can't be overstated—it is inside this communal alternate that your work can locate new dimensions of that means and impact.

Furthermore, embody the exercise of reflection and mindfulness, recognizing that innovative fitness is as vital as bodily fitness to your sturdiness and productivity as an artist. Make self-care a priority; the perception that a balanced existence enhances creativity no longer detracts from it.

Most importantly, commit to an attitude of non-stop learning and growth. The panorama of creativity is ever-changing, with new technologies, ideas, and challenges rising at each and every turn. Stay curious, stay adaptable, and by no means lose the ardor for exploration that drives the coronary heart of each proper artist.

This name to motion is no longer simply a conclusion to an e-book, but the opening of a new chapter in your innovative life. It's an encouragement to take the reins of your creative journey, to steer it with intention and courage, and to include the endless probabilities that lie ahead.

As you shut this e-book and step lower back into the world, lift with you the information that creativity is no longer a vacation spot but a way of living. It's a route marked by non-stop discovery, relentless passion, and the unyielding pursuit of expression. The equipment is in your hands, the map was laid out earlier than you, and the experience is yours to command. So, take a deep breath, set your sights on the horizon, and let the journey begin.

Looking to the Future

As we stand at the precipice of tomorrow, looking at the large expanse of the unknown, the ultimate chapter of this experience beckons us ahead with a message of hope, aspiration, and boundless possibility. "Looking to the Future" is no longer only a conclusion but also a commencement—a beginning factor for the subsequent leg of your innovative odyssey. It is an invitation to view the horizon no longer as a restriction but as a promise of endless potential, a reminder that the direction of creativity stretches a way past what the eye can see.

The future of your innovative experience is a canvas but unpainted, a story but unwritten, and a melody but unsung. It is ripe with possibilities for growth, innovation, and exploration. Embrace this open-endedness with enthusiasm and optimism, for it is in the unknown that the best adventures are located, and the most profound discoveries are made.

As you pass forward, lift with you the training realized from the past, the techniques honed through practice, and the insights received from each success and setback. Let these be your guideposts, illuminating the route as you navigate the ever-evolving panorama of creativity. Remember, the experience of an artist is one of perpetual becoming, a non-stop procedure of reinvention and renewal.

Set your sights on new horizons, daring to dream big and attain the stars. The future holds possibilities for innovative expression that are nowadays unimaginable. Stay open to the chances that emerge from technological advancements, cultural shifts, and the cross-pollination of thoughts and disciplines. The fusion of these factors will spawn new varieties of art, new modes of expression, and new avenues for sharing your work with the world.

Most importantly, view the future with a spirit of generosity and collaboration. The innovative ride is no longer a solitary undertaking but rather a shared voyage. By lifting others as you climb, by means of sharing your knowledge, your art, and your heart, you make a contribution to a vibrant, thriving, innovative ecosystem that benefits all who are part of it.

In closing, "Looking to the Future" is a name for boldness, a project to envision a creative lifestyle that is rich, fulfilling, and impactful. It is a reminder that the ride does not stop right here; it continues with every new day, every new project, and every new soar of faith. So, as you flip the web page and step into the unwritten chapters of your innovative life, do so with the bravery to create the resilience to persevere, and the knowledge to evolve. The future is yours to shape, and the world awaits the splendor only you can carry to life.

Appendices

Supplementary Resources

Constant in nature is the pursuit of knowledge and inspiration throughout the creative process. In order to assist you in your investigation, we have compiled the subsequent inventory of curated resources—books, websites, and platforms—that provide comprehensive analyses of the domains of innovation, art, and creativity.

"The Artist's Way" authored by Julia Cameron is a seminal work that provides a comprehensive 12-week program for individuals to rediscover their creative potential.

An invigorating perspective on creativity, "Steal Like an Artist" by Austin Kleon urges artists to embrace influence and reimagine the world.

Elizabeth Gilbert's "Big Magic: Creative Living Beyond Fear" examines the mindsets, strategies, and routines that enable us to lead the most imaginative and productive lives possible.

A guide to identifying and cultivating creativity, "Creative Confidence" by Tom Kelley and David Kelley serves as an instrument to release the creative potential that resides within each individual.

Websites: Behance (behance.net): An all-access platform for showcasing and discovering interdisciplinary creative work.

A wide array of presentations on creativity, innovation, and design delivered by esteemed scholars and professionals can be found on TED (ted.com).

Many of the online courses offered by universities around the globe on Coursera (coursera.org) pertain to design and creativity.

An compendium of cross-disciplinary interest that spans art, science, design, history, and philosophy, among others, is Brain Pickings (brainpickings.org).

Platforms: Pinterest (pinterest.com) serves as a repository of ideas and inspiration for initiatives spanning diverse creative domains.

CreativeLive (creativelive.com) provides seminars led by industry experts in photography, art, design, audio, and other disciplines.

Creative Practices

In order to enhance the incorporation of the principles explored in this literary work into one's creative endeavors, the following set of exercises has been meticulously crafted to ignite inspiration and cultivate development.

Good morning, newspapers: Compose three pages of stream-of-consciousness each morning. This "The Artist's Way" exercise facilitates the elimination of mental debris and the discovery of creative concepts.

Concept Journal: Constantly carry a small notebook or a digital application with you in order to record inspiration, ideas, or sketches that occur throughout the day.

The Remix Competition: Reproduce an artwork that you hold in high regard into a new piece of your own. This may entail composing a narrative motivated by a painting or generating an artistic creation influenced by a composition of music.

Limitations on Creativity: Establish a constraining creative challenge, such as the following: compose a narrative in 100 words or produce an artwork utilizing exclusively three colors. Constraints frequently stimulate innovation by requiring one to ponder in a limited space.

Engage in an observational stroll through your local community, dedicating your time to simply behold your immediate environs.

Attempt to perceive the mundane in a novel way and jot down any imaginative concepts that emerge.

Conducting Interviews with Creative Experts

In order to provide perspectives and counsel from individuals who have effectively traversed their own creative trajectories, this segment comprises interviews with creative experts from an assortment of fields. Every interview explores the individual trajectory of the creative, including the obstacles they have encountered, the approaches they have utilized to maintain their inventiveness and attain accomplishments within their respective domains.

The highlights are:

A novelist explores the significance of routine in surmounting writer's block and its impact on her writing process.

An individual who specializes in visual art recounts his progression from novice to expert, emphasizing the value of tenacity and community assistance.

A music producer discusses the influence of collaboration on his work and the development of his distinctive aesthetic.

These interviews now function not only as a repository of ideas but also as a practical manual, providing practical advice and inspiration to individuals seeking to foster a more profound connection with innovation and forge their own distinctive trajectory.

www.ingramcontent.com/pod-product-compliance
Lightning Source LLC
Chambersburg PA
CBHW020838150726
48196CB00002B/116